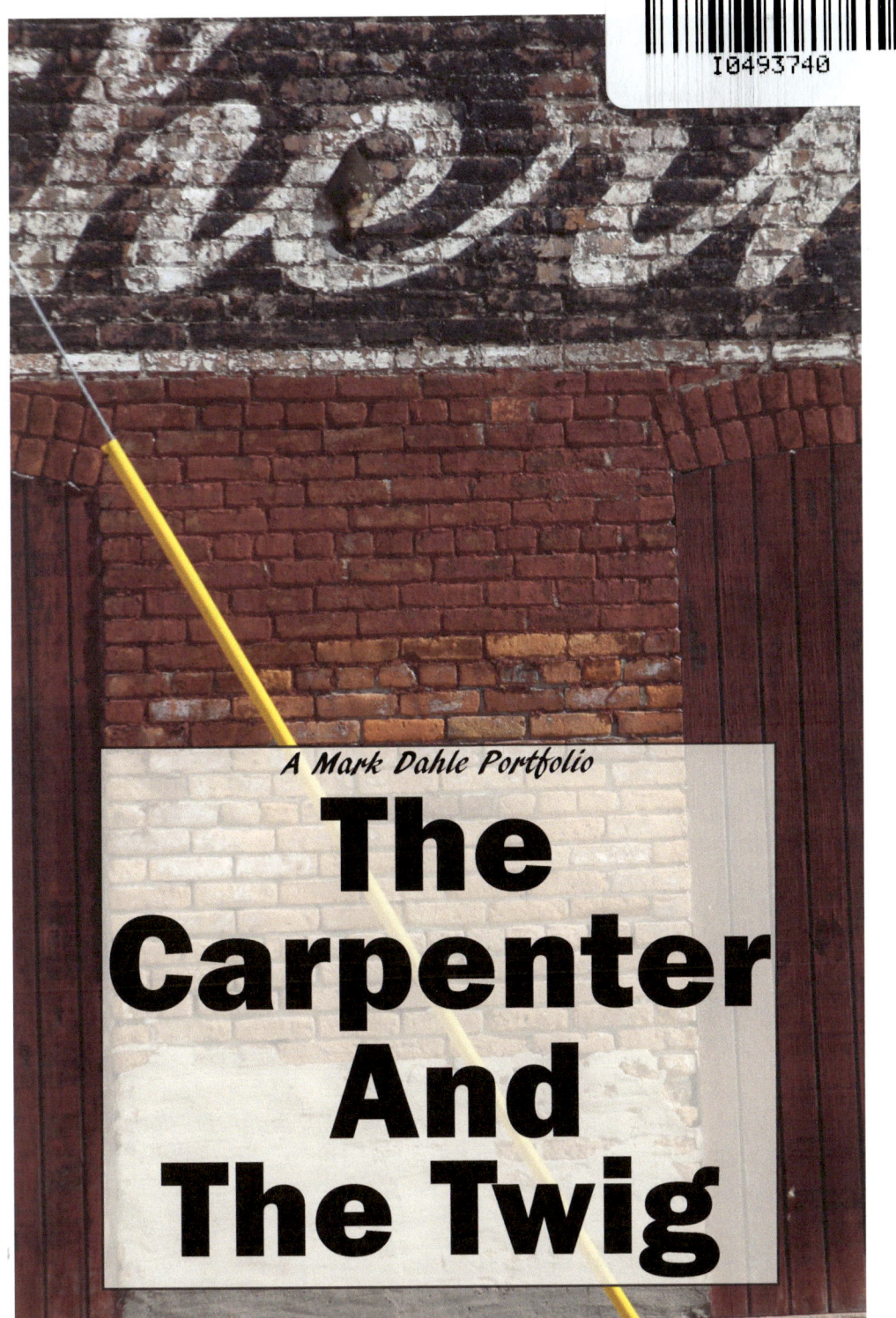

A Mark Dahle Portfolio

The Carpenter And The Twig

Mark Dahle Portfolios can be read in a few minutes and enjoyed for a lifetime.

Unlike many picture books, the text is not related to the beautiful painting at the right and the photographs that follow. This might seem a little weird at first. One thing that helps is to order more portfolios until you get used to it. In the meantime, feel free to draw your own pictures of fine furniture made from scraps if you like.

This portfolio includes a photo of a brilliant 36 x 24 inch painting (at the right), twenty-six beautiful photos of Detroit, Michigan, and a story about a carpenter who made fine furniture from scraps.

Photographs in this book are available in very limited editions. See http://www.MarkDahle.com for more information and for previews of upcoming portfolios.

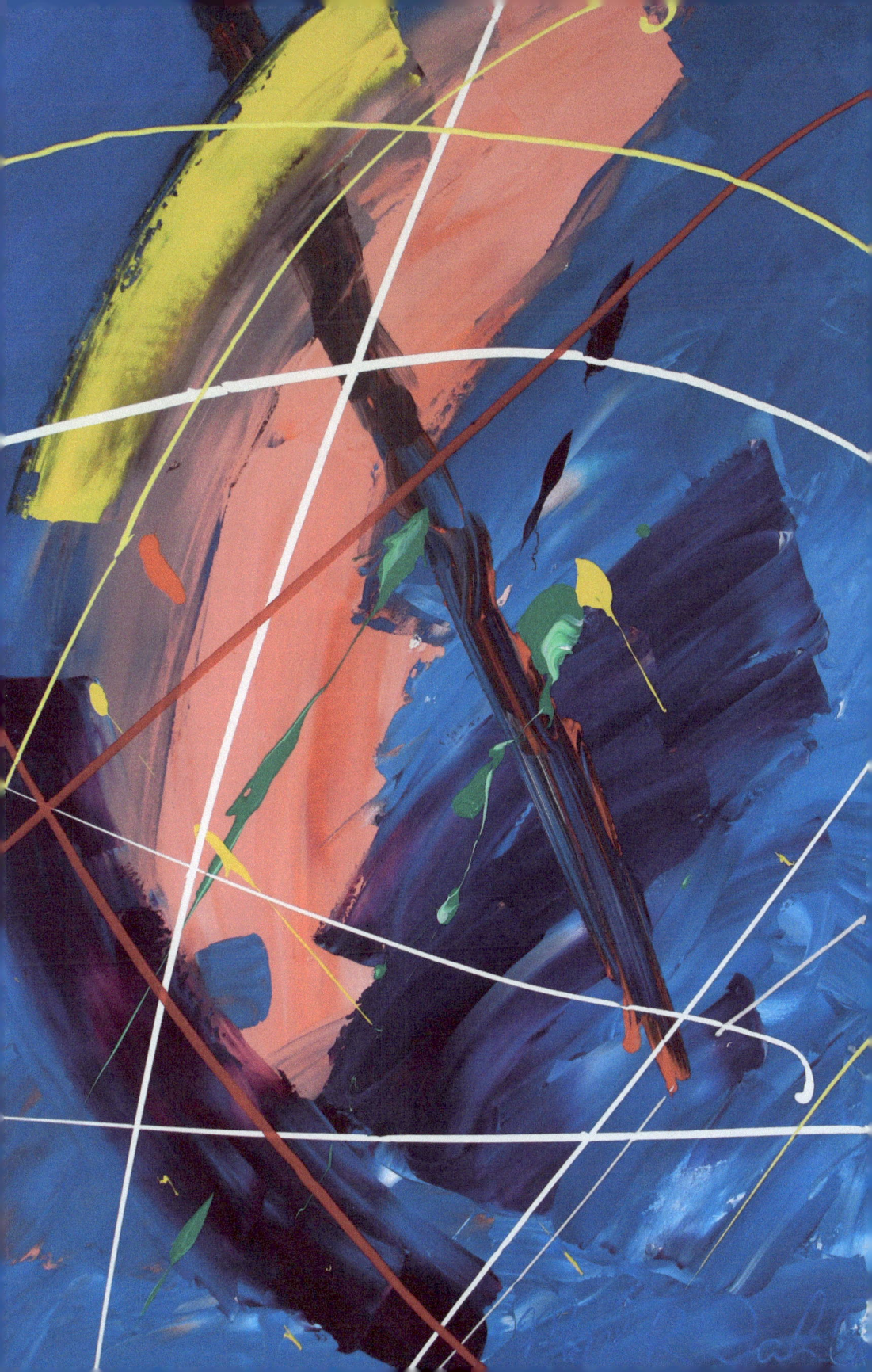

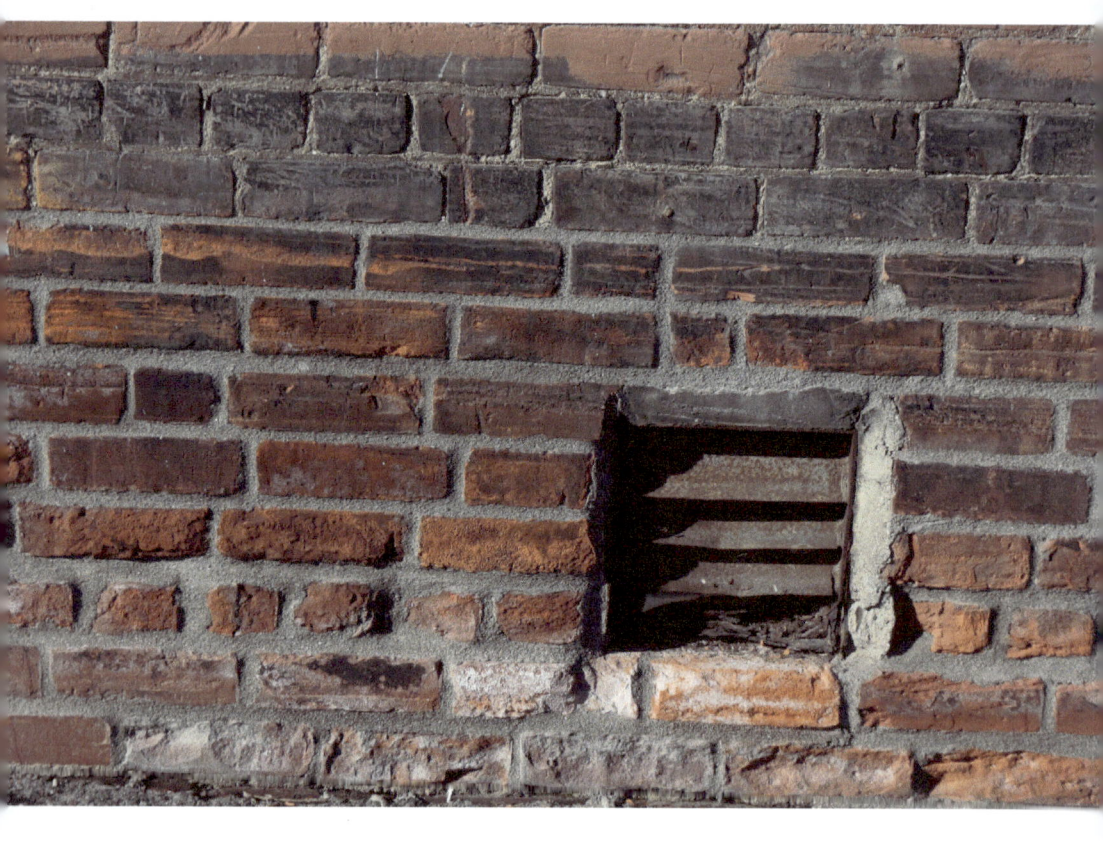

Once there was a carpenter who was quite poor. He used every scrap object he could find to craft bowls, cabinets, tables, chairs and the like. He could make anything, and he was quite skilled at transforming discarded materials into objects of beauty. Every abandoned fragment he found wound up transformed. All except for one lone twig.

The carpenter came across the twig one day while scouring the countryside for debris. He had already found a sheet of plastic, a broken piece of plywood and several rusty, bent nails. Those he knew he could use. But the twig? He could not imagine a use for it. Nevertheless, it caught his attention as he walked along the edge of a forest. He absentmindedly picked it up.

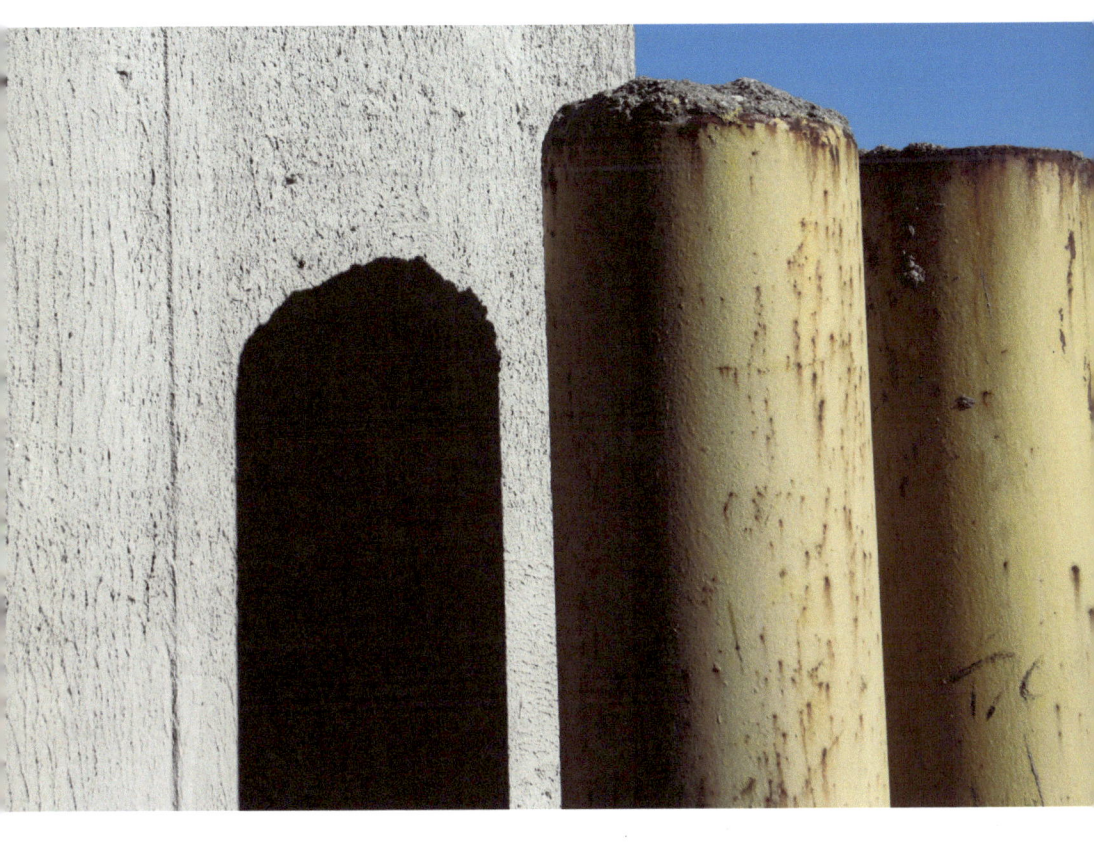

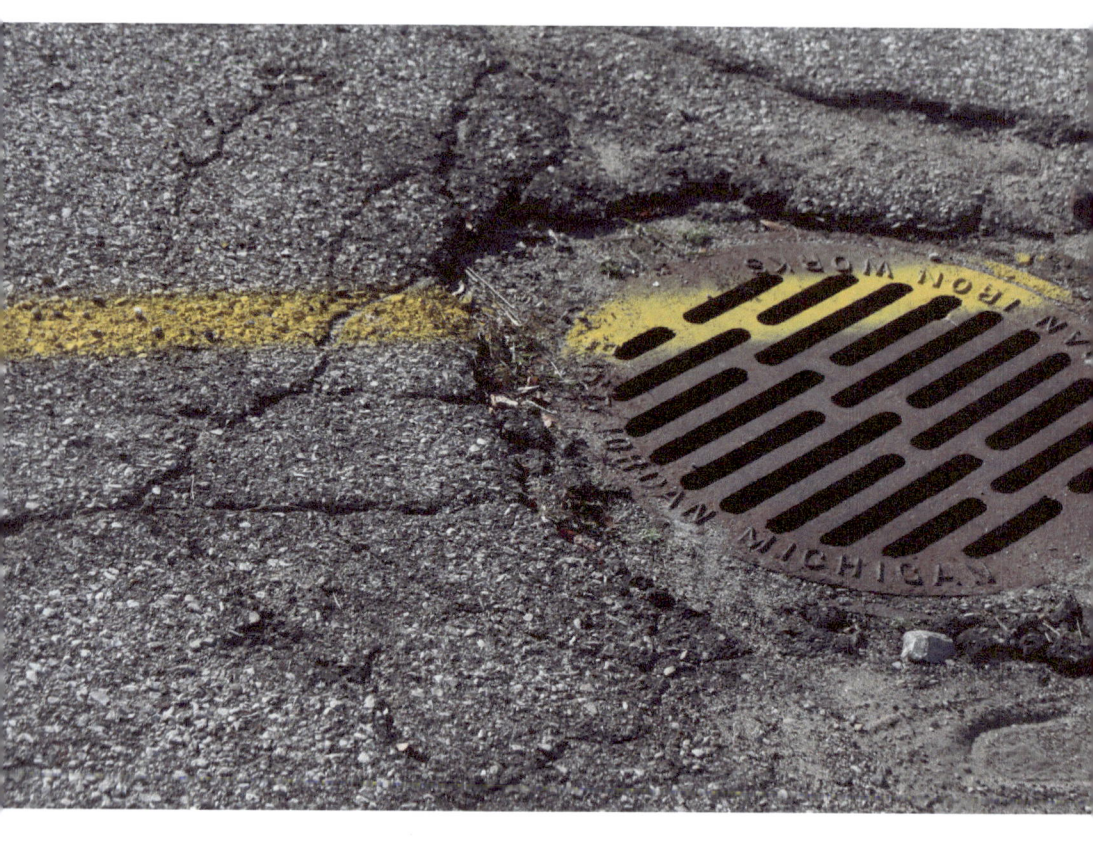

When he got home, the carpenter put the twig against the wall in a corner of his workshop near the stove. For several days he made beautiful objects out of the other materials he had scavenged. And all that week as he selected scraps to work with, he looked at the twig and wondered why it had caught his eye and what he might make of it.

A year passed. On most days the twig had been easily forgotten, as the carpenter's friends brought him scraps of material whenever they could. Some days the twig was completely buried by the debris they had brought. But sometimes it was the only unused material left in the shop. And after a year, the carpenter still had no idea how to use it.

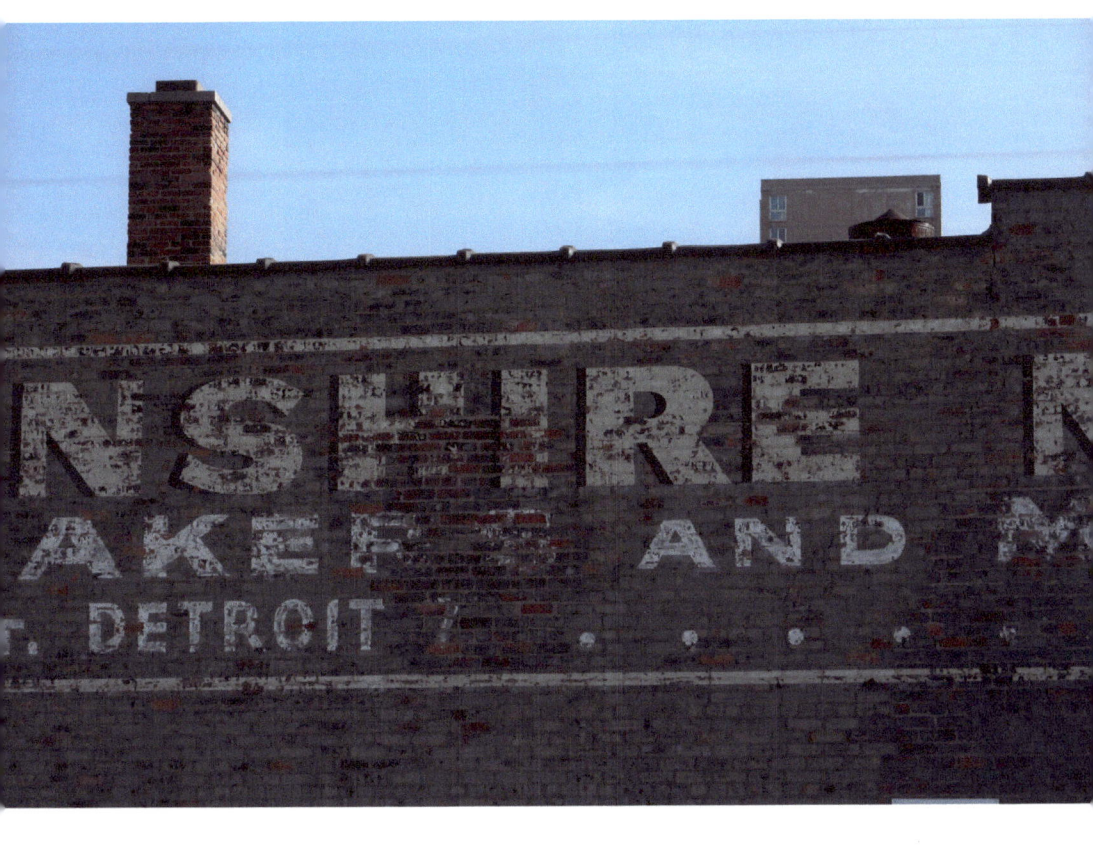

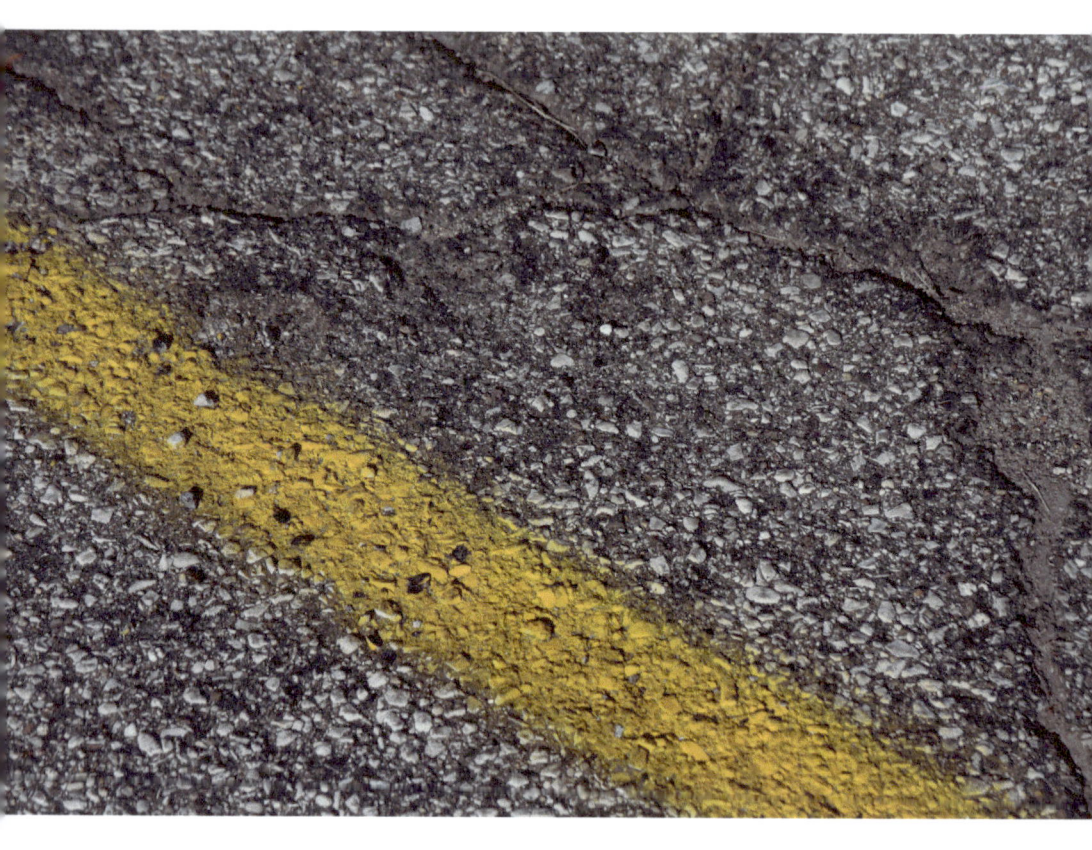

One day the king surprised the carpenter with a visit. The king had heard of the carpenter's fine work with broken materials and he had a special request.

"My daughter is growing proud and selfish," the king confided. "Her birthday is in six weeks. I want to give her something made from scraps – something beautiful – but something to show her there is value in humble things. Can you do that for me?"

The carpenter would never have refused the king. He promised he would make her a suitable present.

"Excellent," said the king. "I will be back in six weeks and pick up the gift on the way to her party."

In spite of his promise, the carpenter had no idea what he could make that would be suitable for the king's daughter.

By chance, a windstorm two days later provided the carpenter with many materials. For three weeks, the carpenter crafted beautiful chairs and dressers and cabinets from the debris. All were exquisite, perfect for the homes of the carpenter's neighbors. But none seemed just right for the king's request.

What could he make for the king's daughter? The carpenter pondered night and day. When only two weeks were left, he still did not have the present ready.

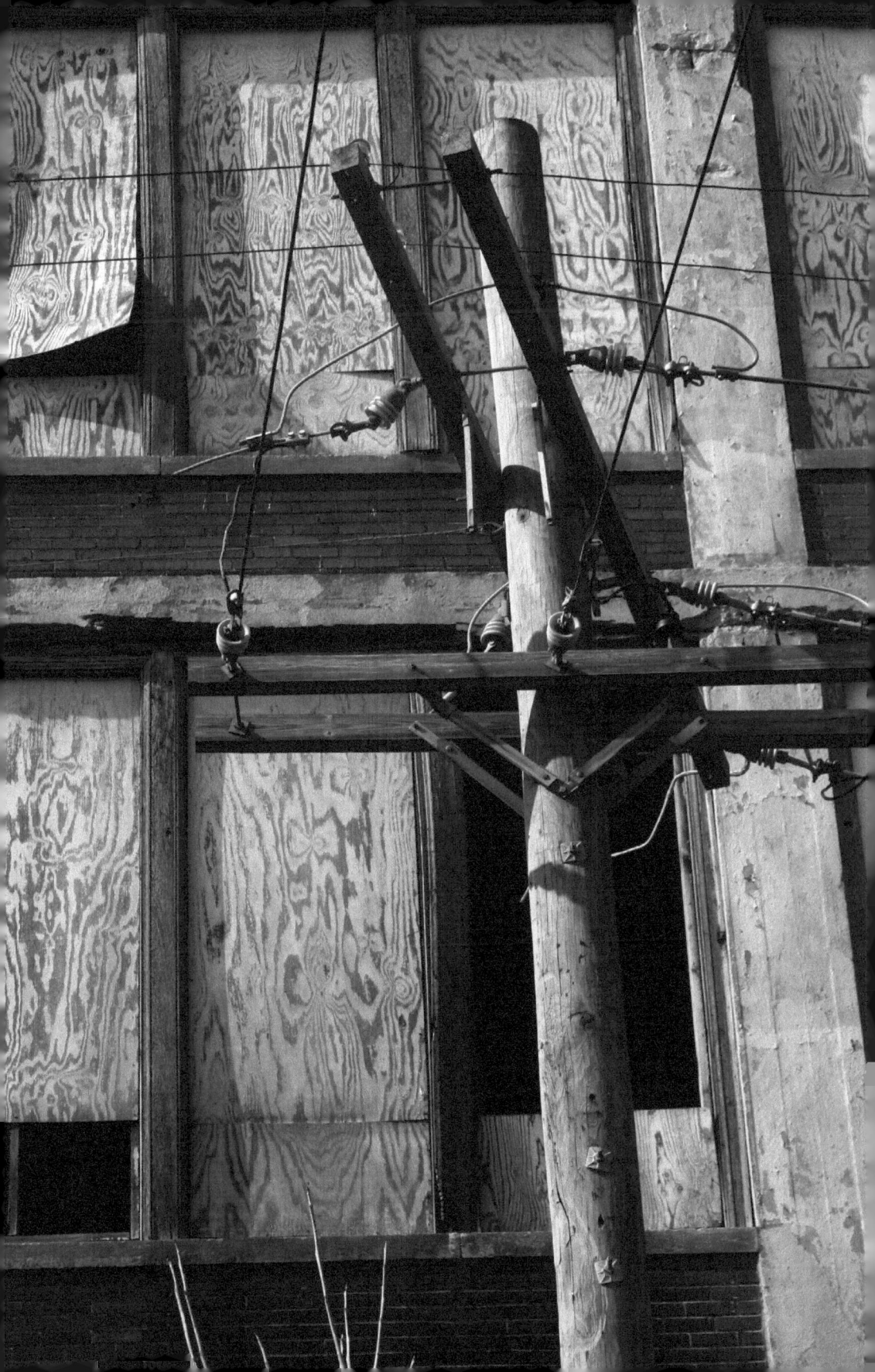

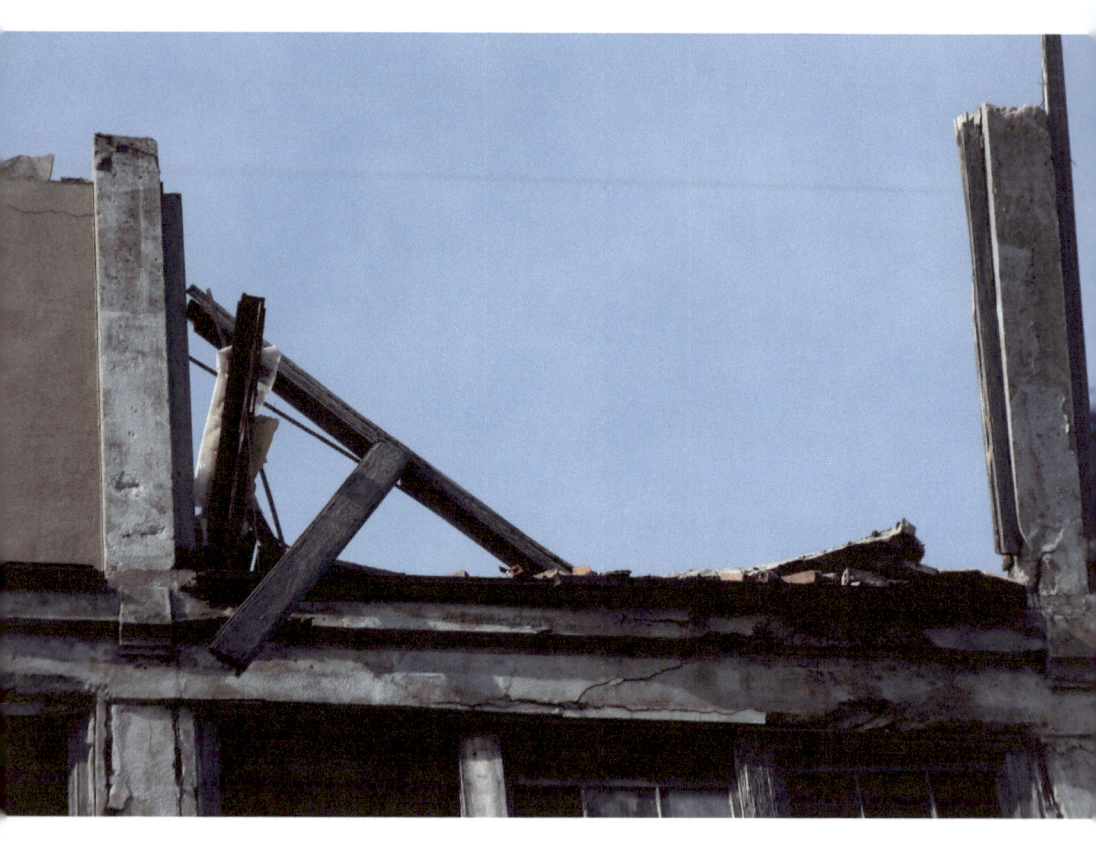

Twelve days before the king would return, a fire in a nearby town burned a factory, and the carpenter had several neighbors help him bring back cartloads of debris. He worked night and day and created some extraordinary pieces of beautiful and useful furniture from the remnants of the fire. But still nothing seemed suitable for the king's request.

With only one day before the king would return, the carpenter was in distress. He was surrounded by finely crafted furniture, but nothing seemed special enough for the king's daughter.

The carpenter tossed and turned all night and at last fell into a fitful sleep. He dreamed a fairy came to his workshop and left her wand in the corner by the stove as a gift for the princess.

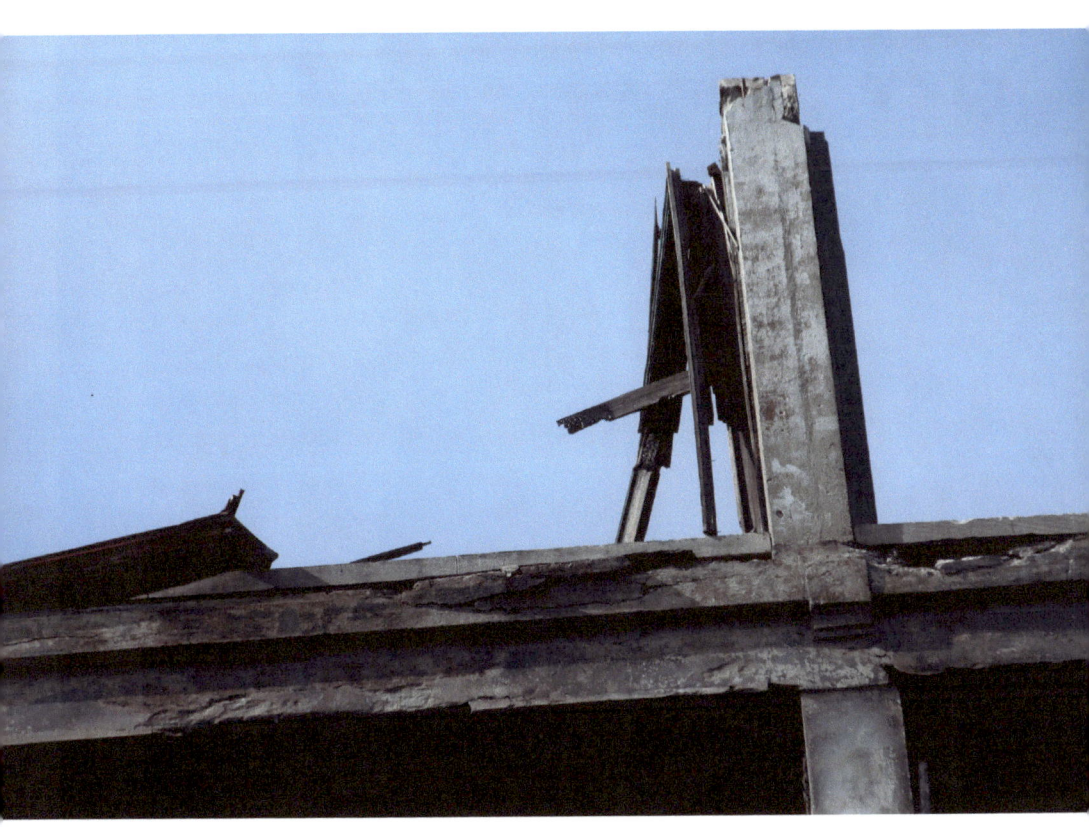

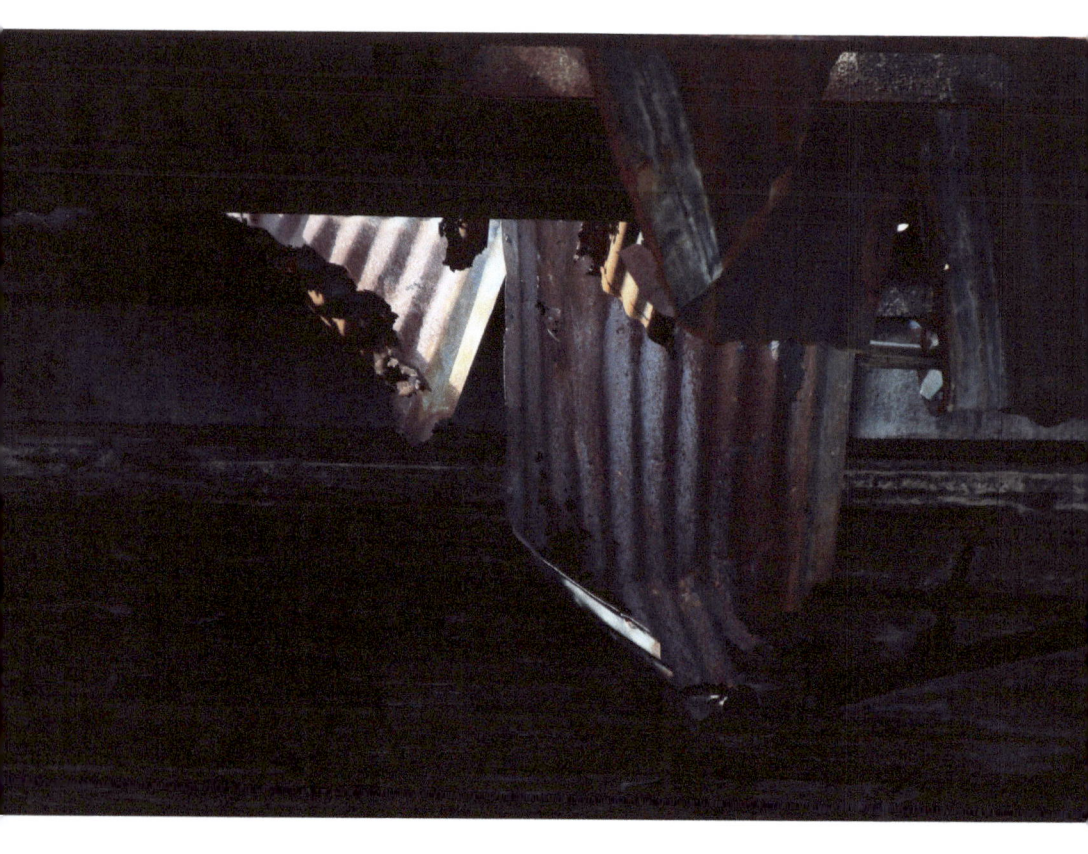

When the carpenter awoke, he rushed to the corner of his shop to see if the dream were true – and there, resting where he had placed it a year before, was the twig.

The carpenter eyed the twig skeptically, but at last he picked it up, wrapped it in scraps of festive paper and tied the package with a red ribbon that he worked into a beautiful bow.

The carpenter fretted all morning. Was the twig good enough for what the king wanted?

By the time the king arrived that afternoon, the carpenter had lost confidence in the package he had wrapped so carefully – it was only a twig. Instead he asked the king to choose his daughter's present.

"You may have anything in my shop that you want," he said.

The king carefully inspected the cabinets and dressers and chairs and tables and bowls and even some toys – all exquisitely made of rubbish, rubbish turned into beautiful objects by the carpenter's skillful hands. The king was very, very impressed with everything crafted by the carpenter, but none of the potential gifts seemed to be just right.

"These are all lovely," the king said. "I see why you have such a good reputation. But I need help choosing. None looks quite right. What do you recommend?"

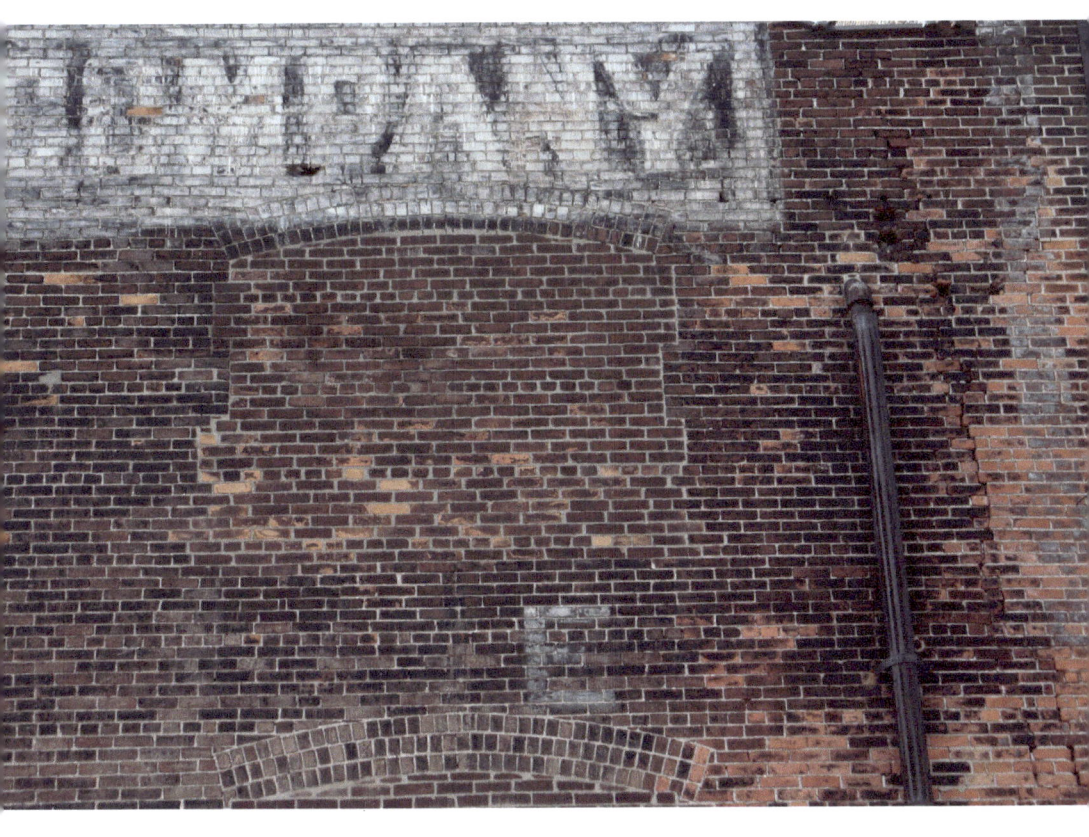

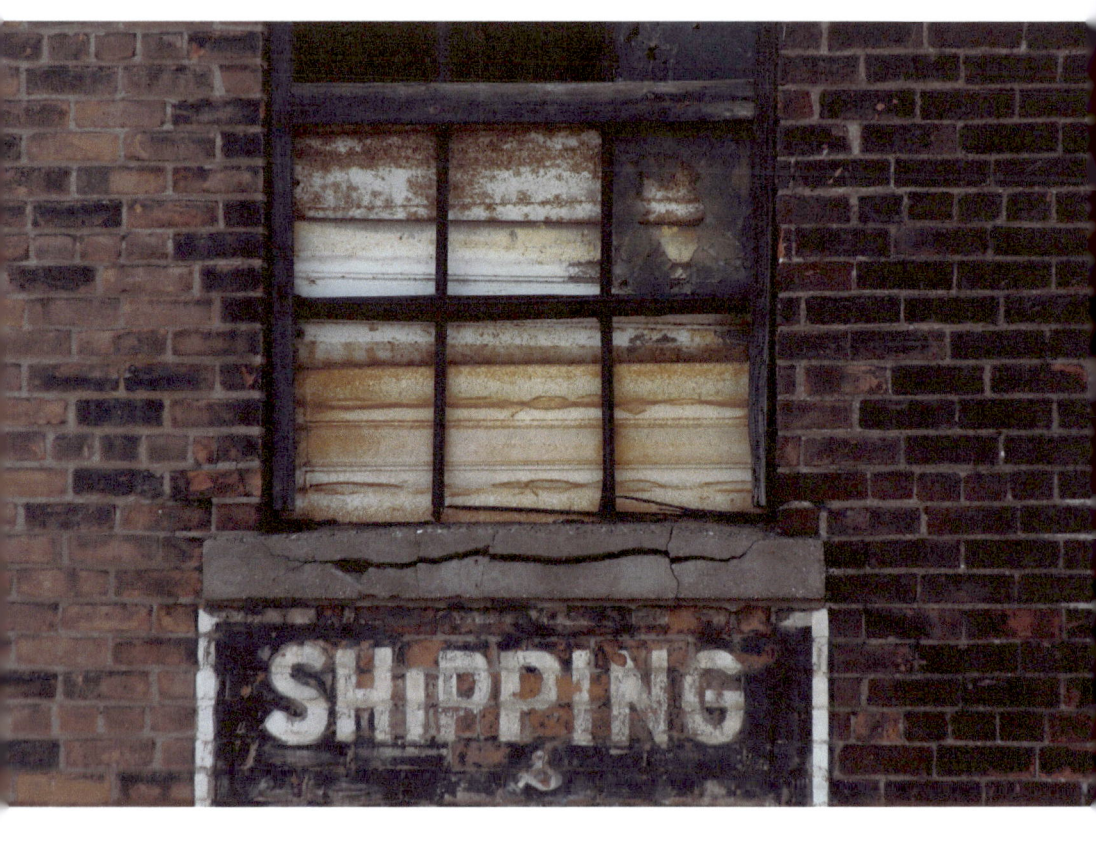

The carpenter almost selected the most beautiful of the dressers for the king, hoping it would be good enough. But at the last second the carpenter found the courage to trust the dream he'd had the night before.

"Here, sire," he said, presenting the king with the twig wrapped in papers and a red ribbon. "This is what I recommend."

The king eyed the package with delight, hefting it, feeling its lightness. "It looks perfect," he said. "What is it?"

"Inside is a magic wand accidentally dropped in the forest by a fairy. I don't know what magic it can do. But it is a very special gift."

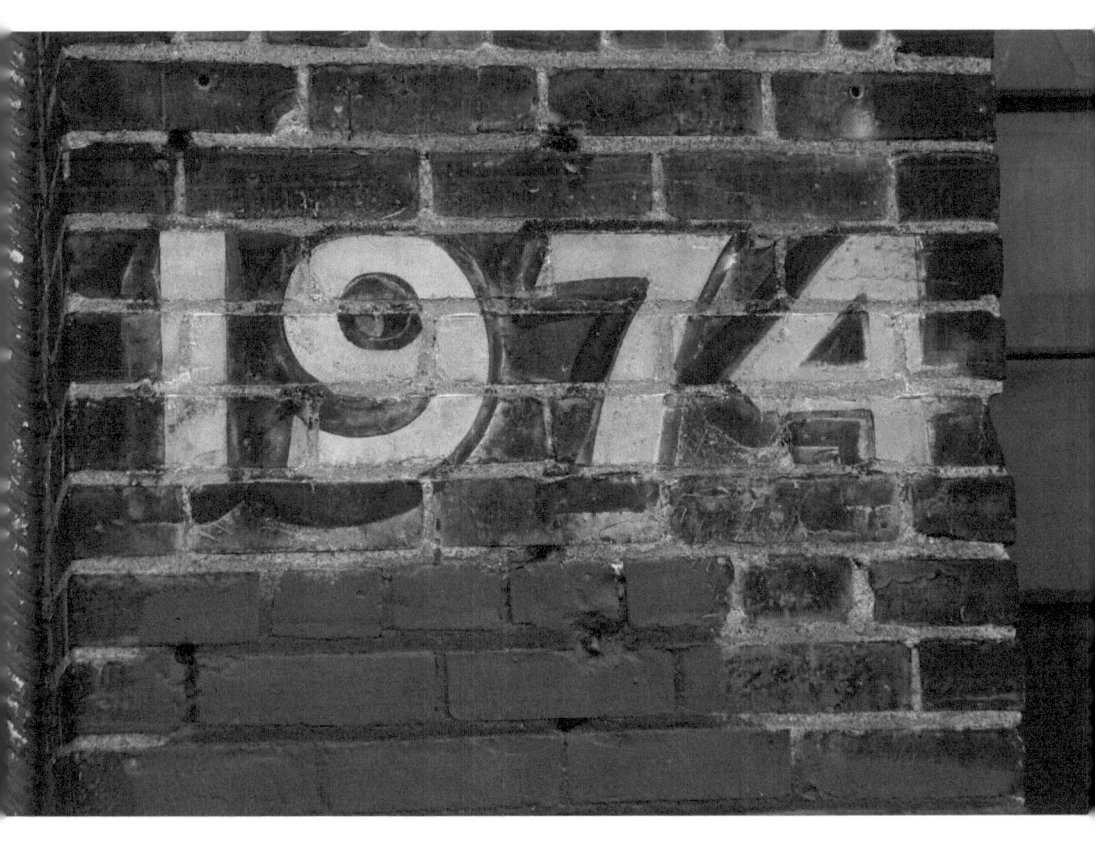

To the carpenter's surprise, the king bowed before him in thanks.

"You honor me with such a priceless gift, and you honor my kingdom with such wonderful furniture that you craft for your neighbors and friends. Thank you."

Then with another nod of his head, the king left the speechless carpenter and went to his daughter's party.

For a while the carpenter was too stunned to move. The king had bowed! To him! A carpenter!

Then some of the carpenter's elation began to fade, and doubt and worry crept in, soon followed by fear and shame.

What had he done? Had he really just lied to the king? He had said the twig was magical. What would the king do when he found the carpenter had given his only daughter a useless old stick?

The carpenter was on a roller coaster of emotions all day. Sometimes he was deliriously happy – he had finally found a use for the twig! The king had even bowed to him and said he did good work! Then he would come crashing down, and he would think that perhaps he would be beheaded for treachery when the king found the present was nothing more than a useless, common twig from the forest. The carpenter's emotions raced up and down all day, and he was even more restless that night. But at last he fell asleep. He had no more dreams of the fairy.

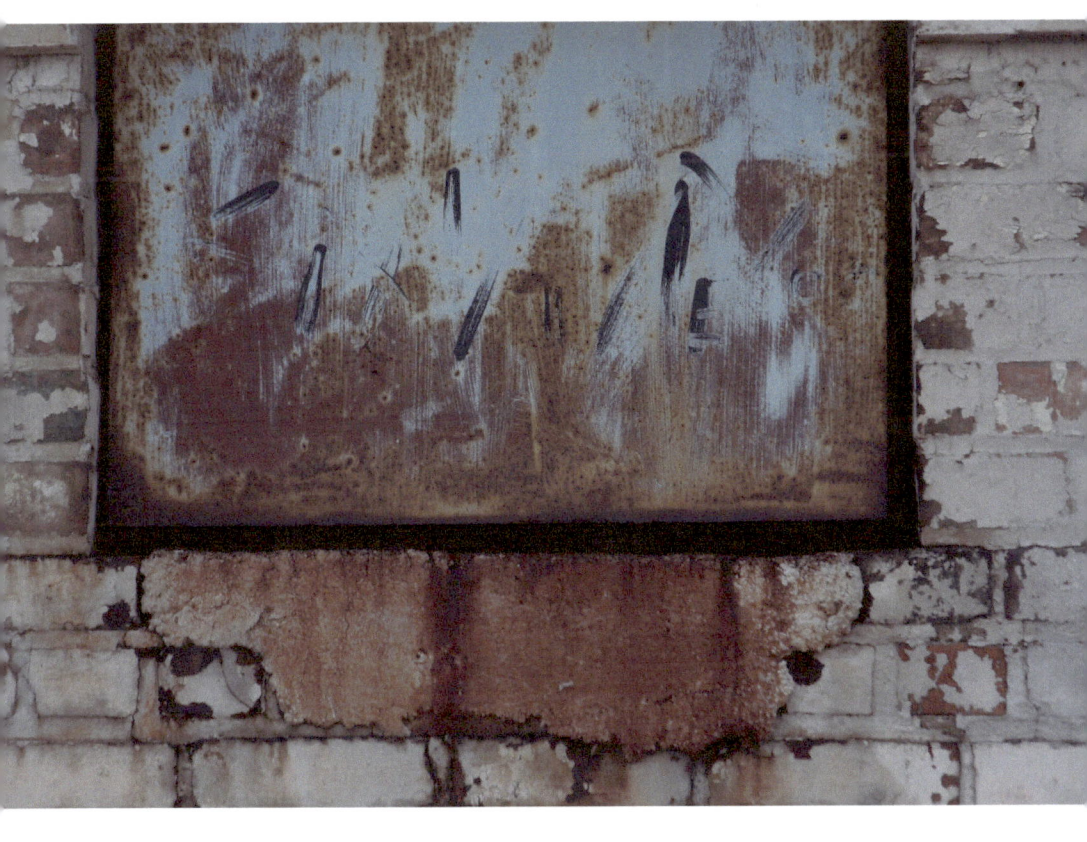

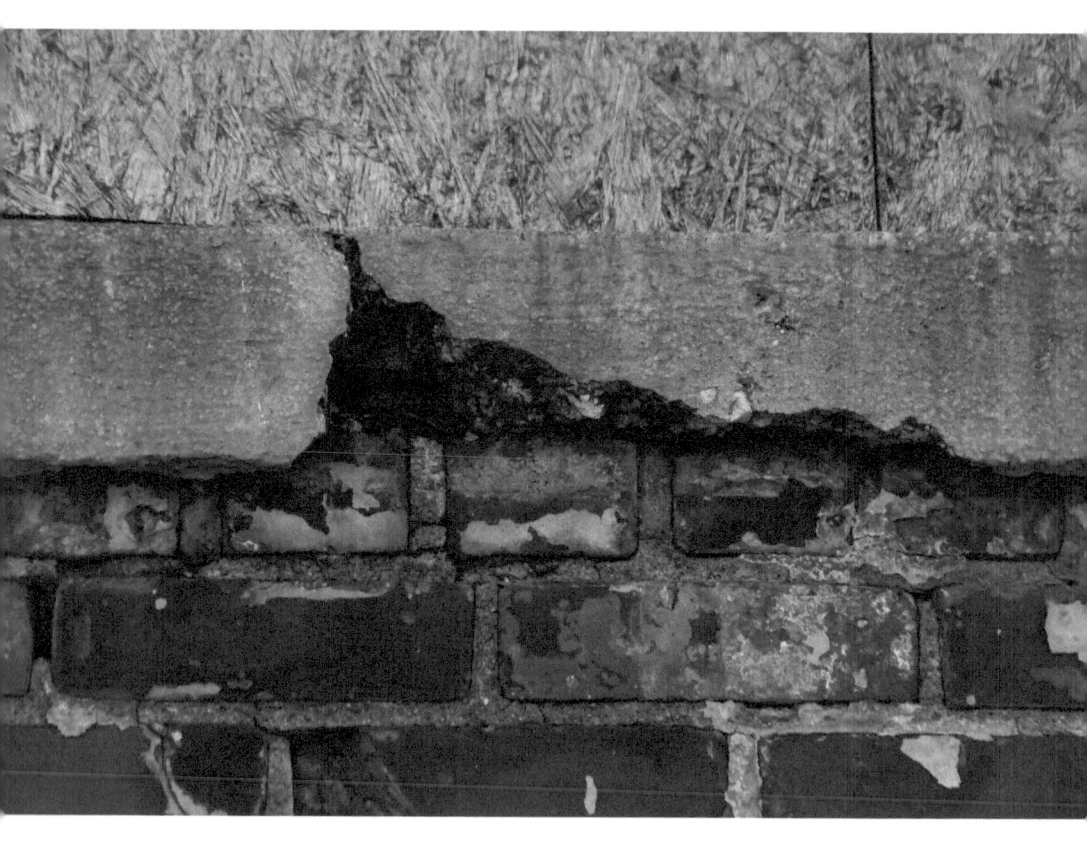

For two weeks the carpenter was alternately anxious and elated, depending on which thoughts he focused on the most. But when he had still not heard any bad reports from the castle after two weeks, he gradually became less afraid and slowly got back to work, creating beautiful objects for his friends and neighbors out of whatever materials he could find.

Another year went by. One day the carpenter received a request from the king for some of the carpenter's furniture. The king paid far more than the carpenter thought possible. It was so much, the carpenter had a hard time believing his good fortune.

The carpenter still worried about the twig from time to time, and he halfway wondered if the request for furniture was some kind of trap to lure him to the castle so he could be punished. But at last the carpenter decided to deliver the beautifully crafted furniture to the castle himself. "If I die, I die," he thought. "I *must* know what happened to that twig!"

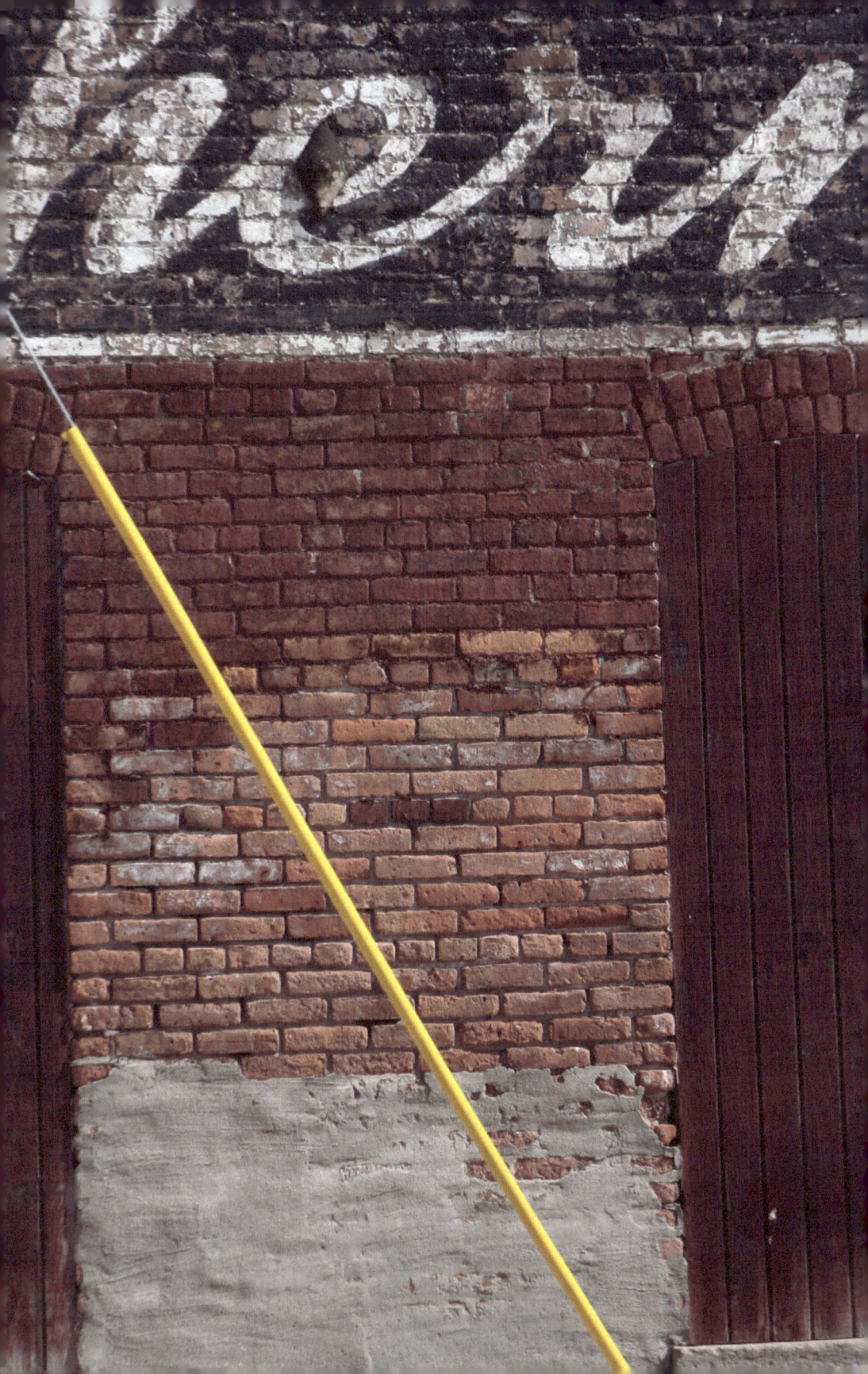

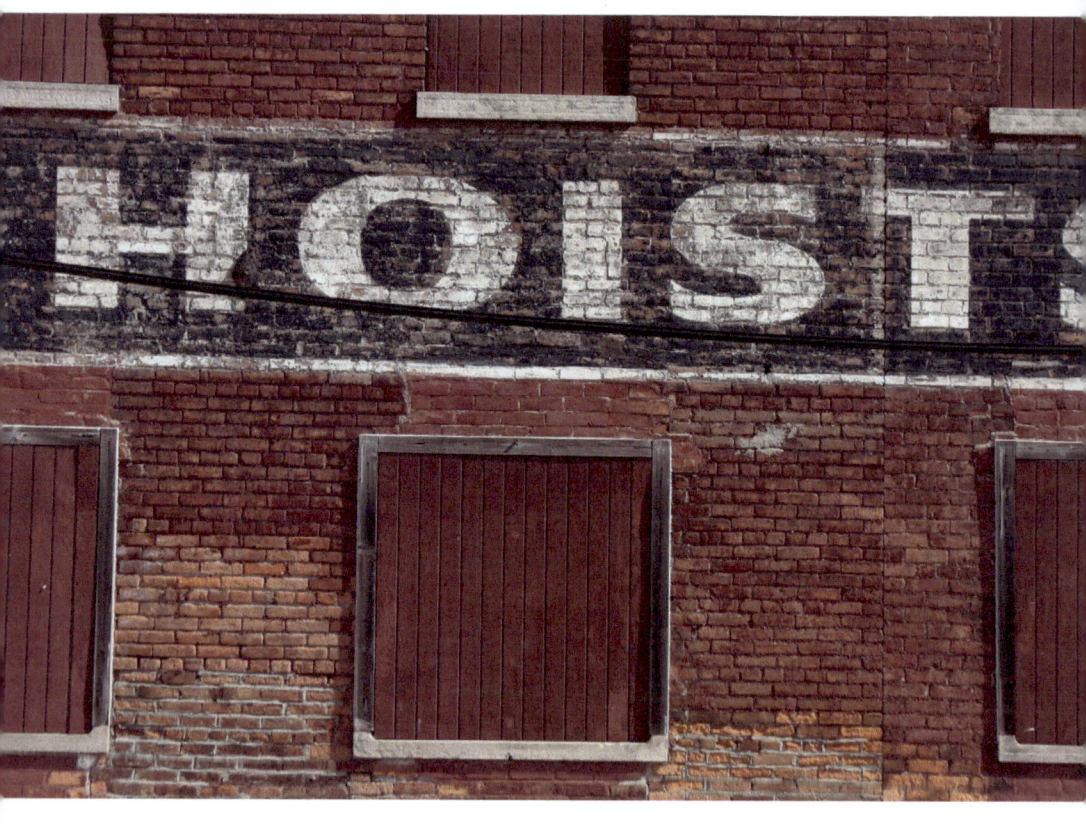

When the carpenter arrived at the castle, he was directed to put all the furniture in a new room in a new wing. The room was being outfitted that day.

"Who will use this room when it is completed?" the carpenter asked one of the servants setting out rugs.

"Don't you know?" she said. "This room belongs to the princess."

The carpenter gasped. He had thought his furniture might be going to some servant's room – perhaps the errand boy of a knight or someone else of very low rank.

"The princess?" he said, startled.

"Yes. She asked for your furniture herself."

"There must be some mistake!" said the carpenter. "I've never met her."

"No," said the servant. "But she's heard all about you. You were the one who crafted her most precious possession."

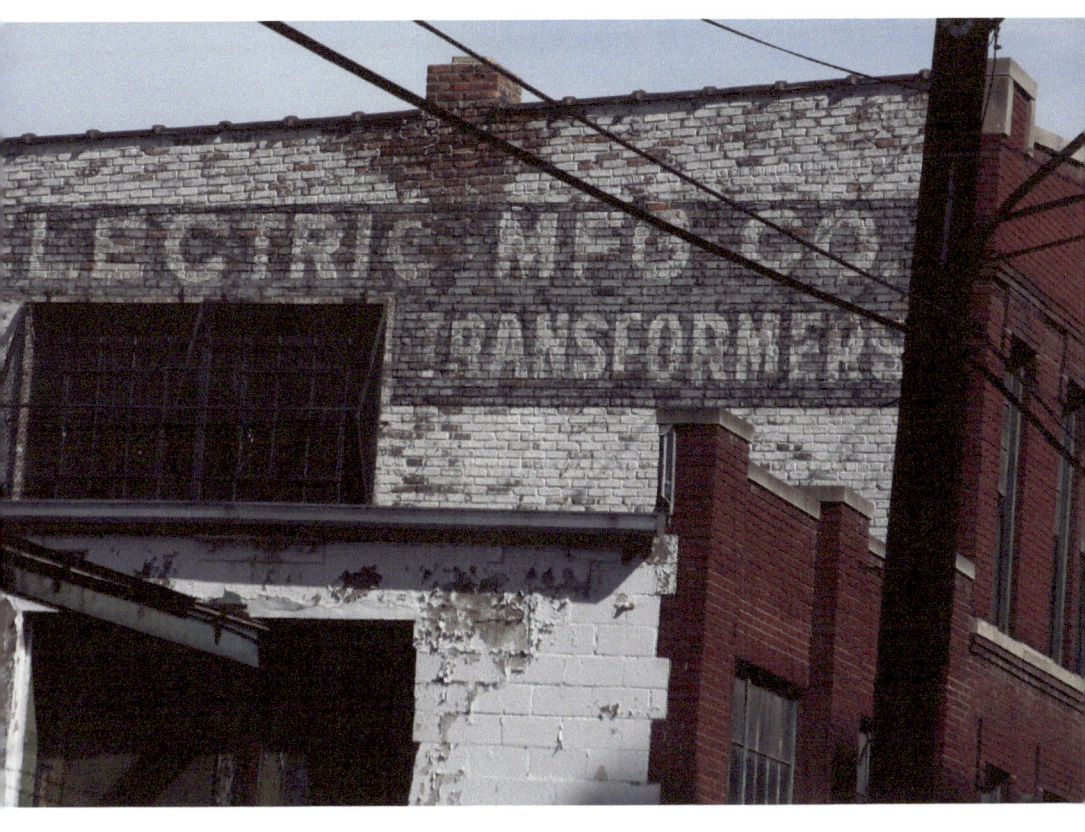

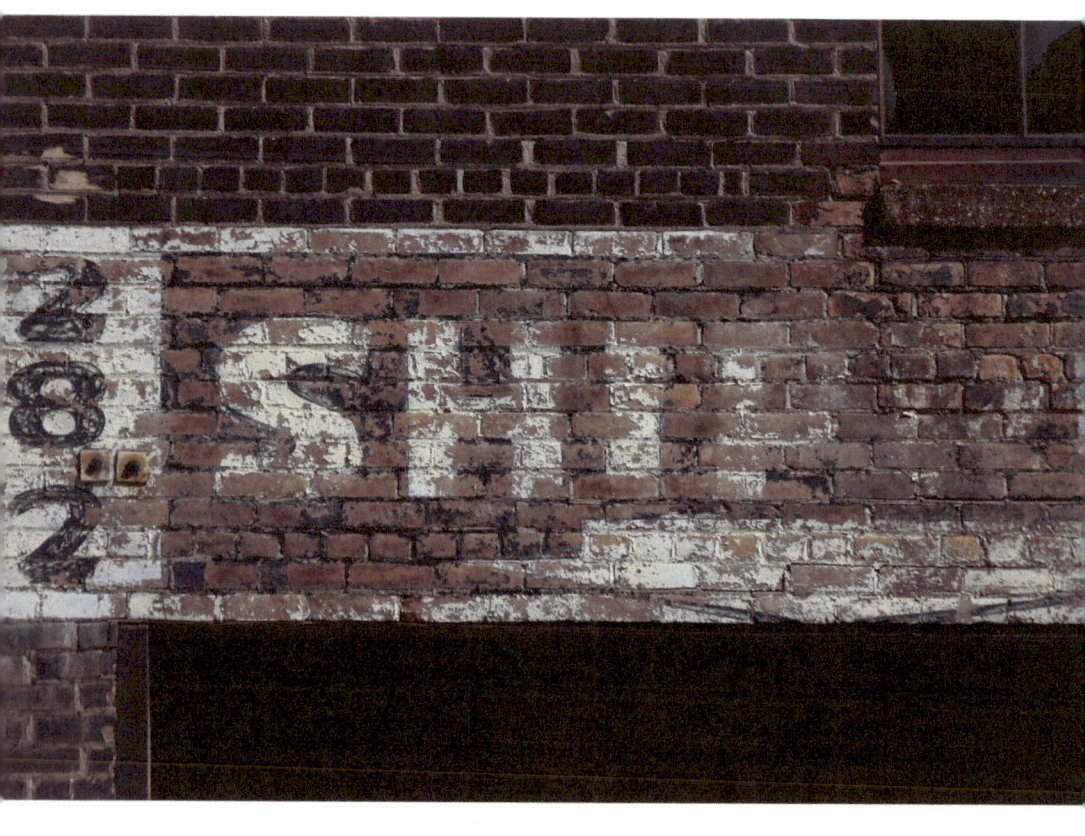

The carpenter was starting to fear for his life again. Surely the servant was making fun of him before telling him the truth and springing the trap.

"I meant no disrespect with the birthday gift," he stammered.

"She loved it," said the servant. "It set her free."

The carpenter looked blankly, then shook his head. "It was just a twig," he said.

"No," said the servant. "It was not just a twig. You took a useless twig – and a story about it – and some festive paper and some red ribbon – to craft something beautiful for the king's daughter. You gave her the gift of imagination. You helped her see that value and magic can be hidden anywhere. The princess has been delighted with your gift all year, and the king could not be more pleased."

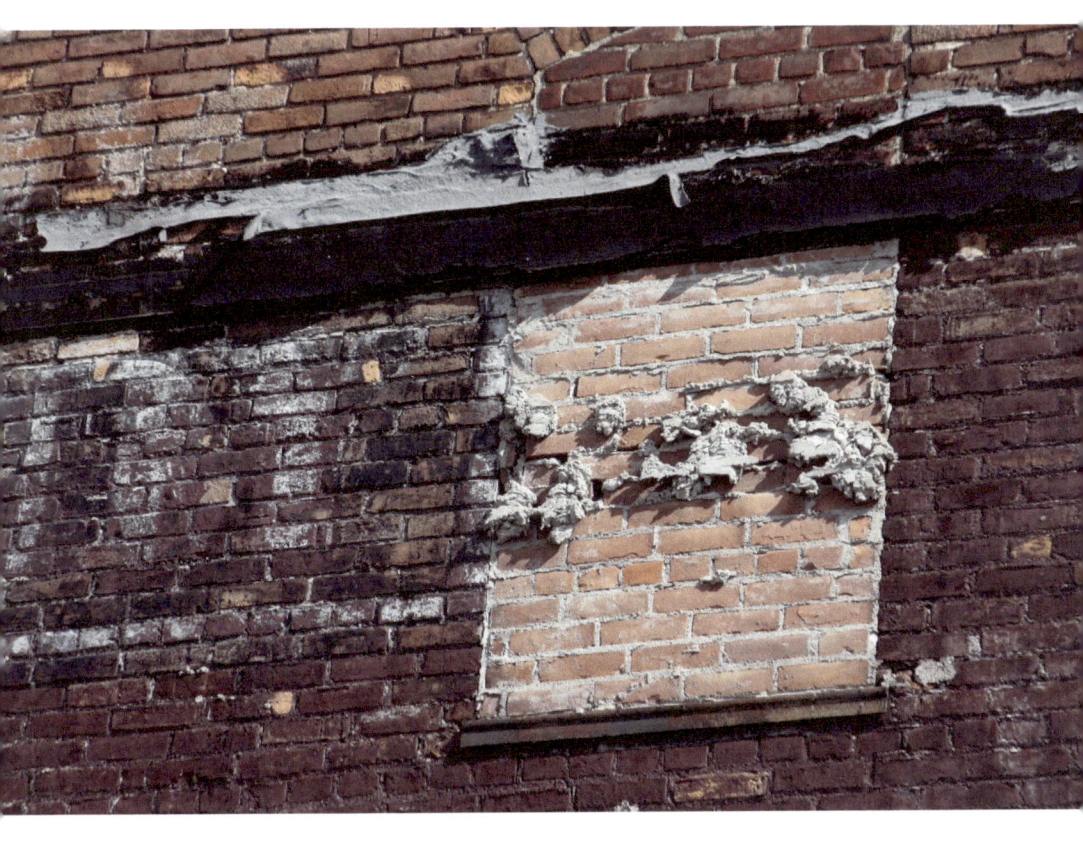

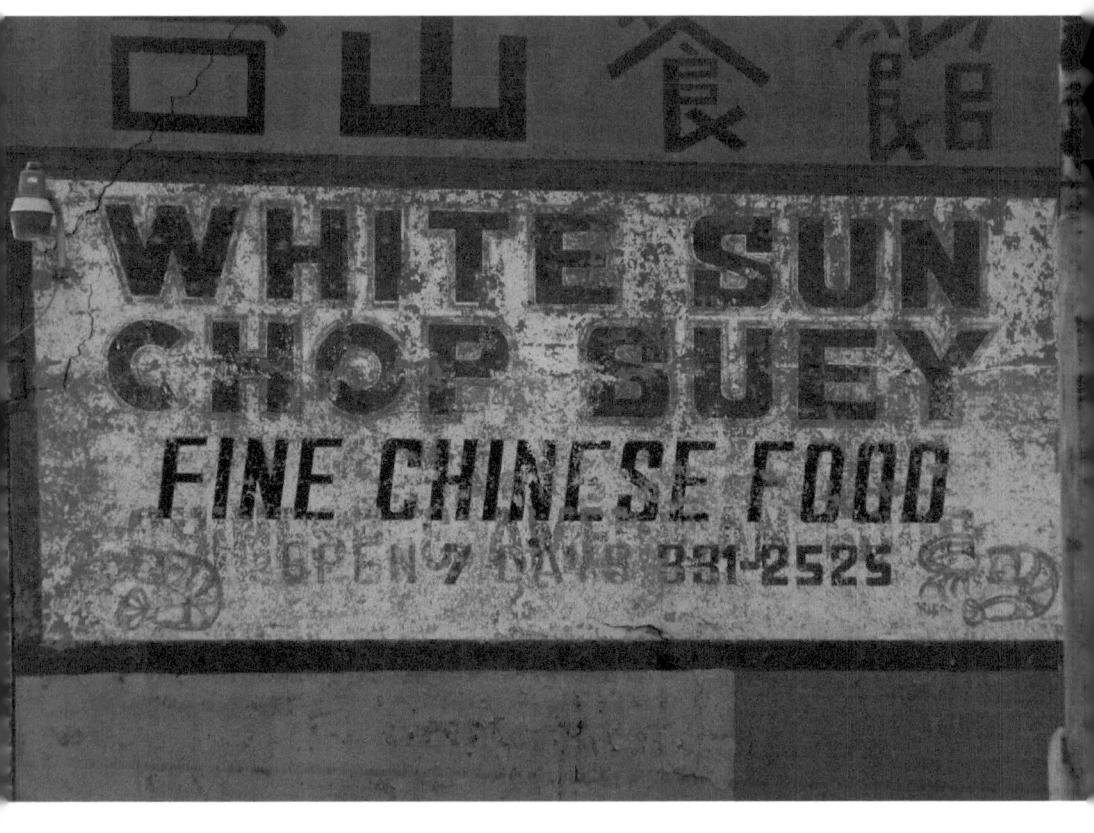

The carpenter left the castle stunned and grateful for his good fortune. It was not until that night when he was dreaming that he realized how much the servant looked like the fairy that had appeared in his dream.

From then on, whenever the carpenter showed people his beautifully crafted furniture, he told stories about it to spark their imaginations.

"You can have the same kind of furniture in your house that the princess selected for her very own bedroom," he told his friends. "Some say it may even be magical." When his friends and neighbors heard that, they began to value their furniture and their homes much more highly, and it gradually transformed the land.

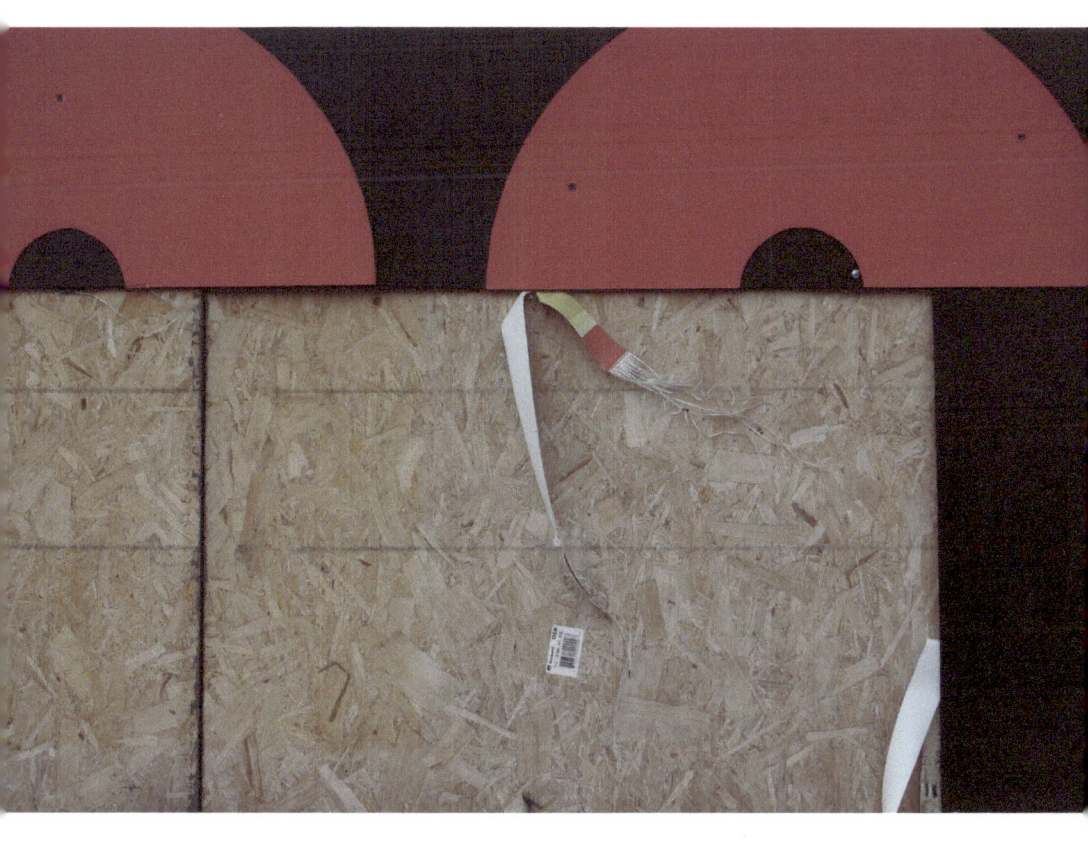

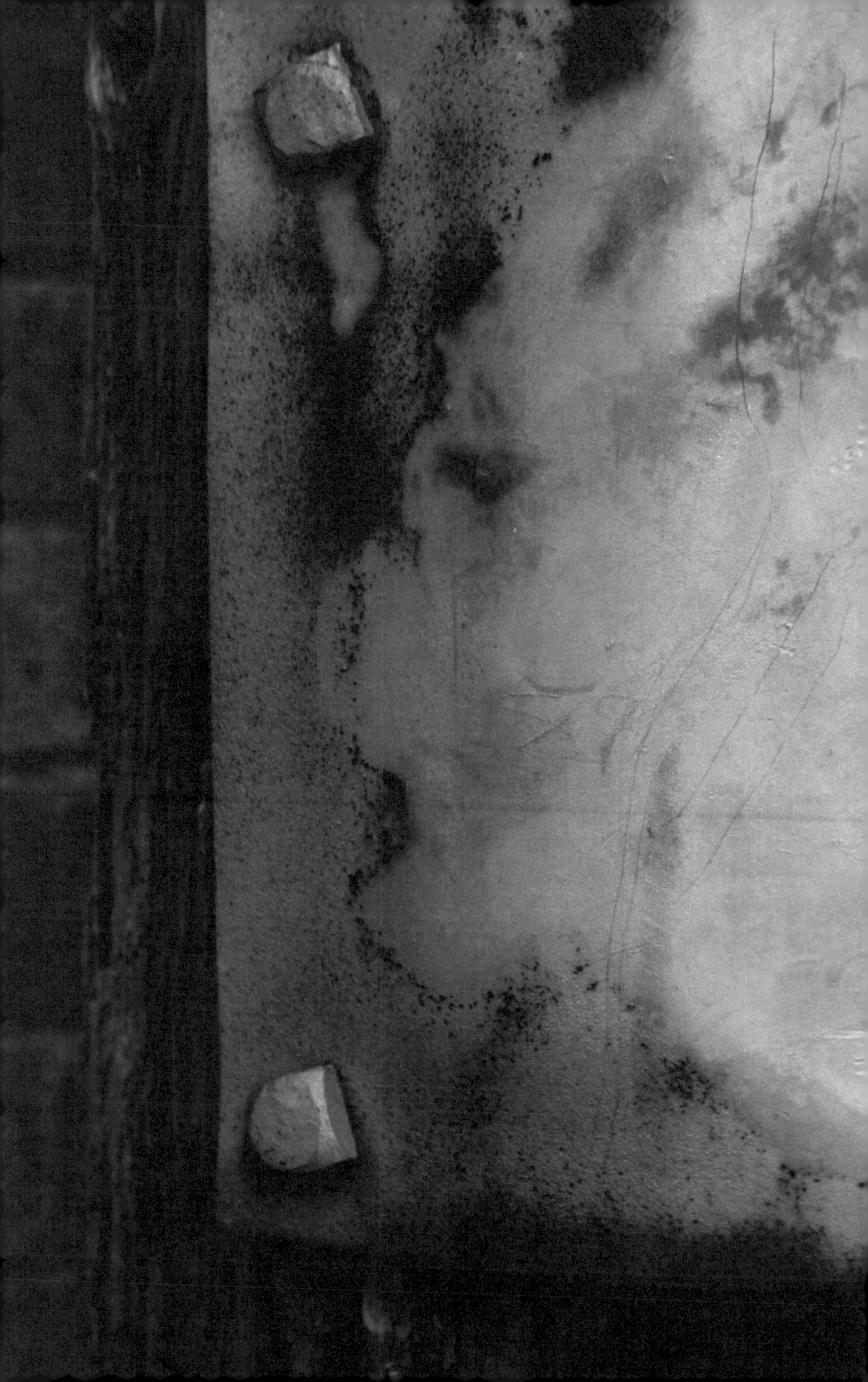

Before the king's visit, the carpenter had offered people very beautiful furniture. But now he offered them very beautiful furniture that gave them confidence and hope and dignity.

Reflection questions

The carpenter was good at making beautiful objects out of debris. What kinds of things are *you* good at?

One day the carpenter discovered he could make things not only by crafting them with his hands but also by telling a story about them. The carpenter did nothing to the twig except present it well (with wrapping paper and a ribbon) and tell a story about its origins. What can you improve by saying something special about it?

What good words might you offer that would cause your neighbors and friends to value their houses, businesses and communities more highly?

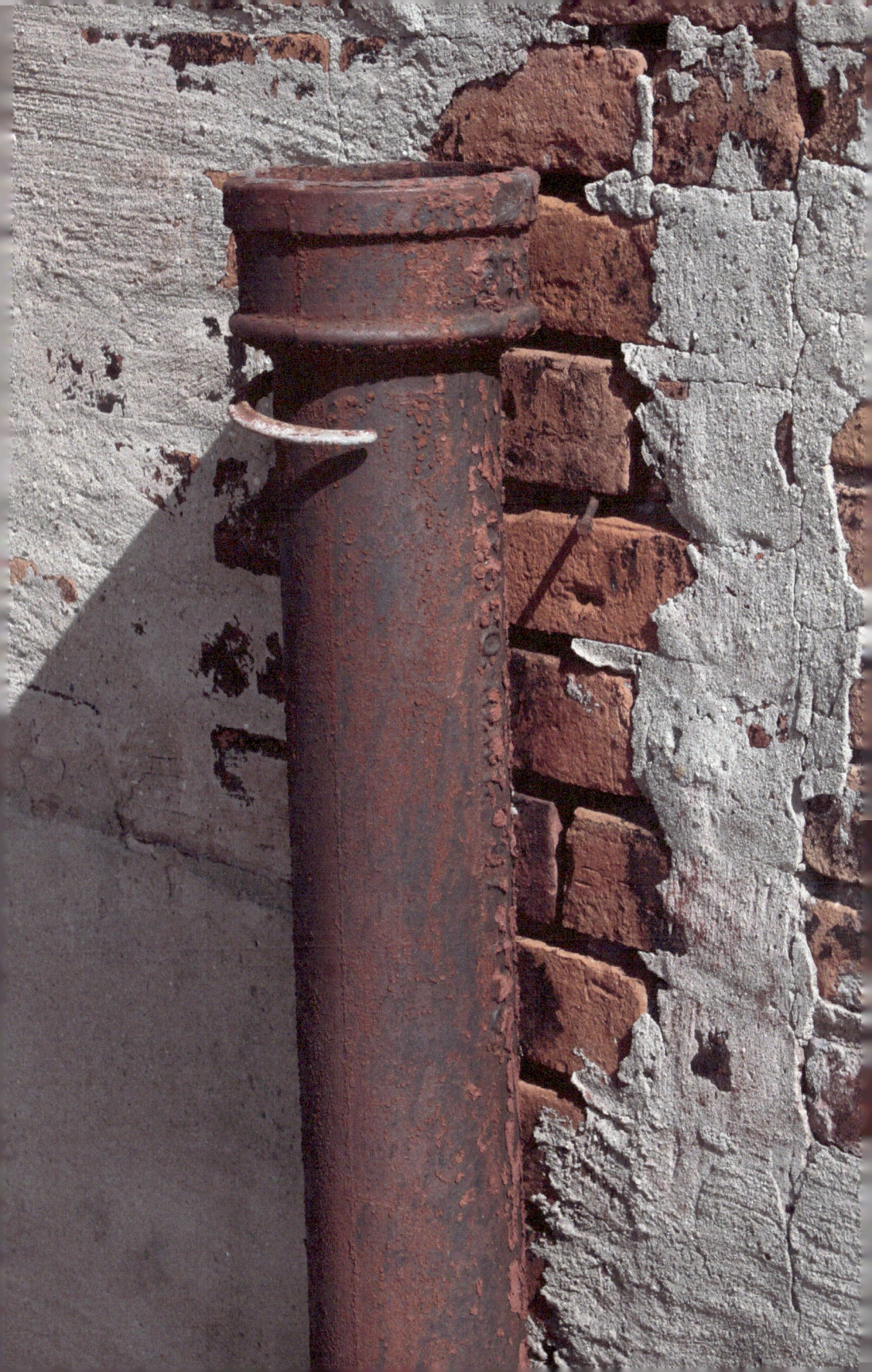

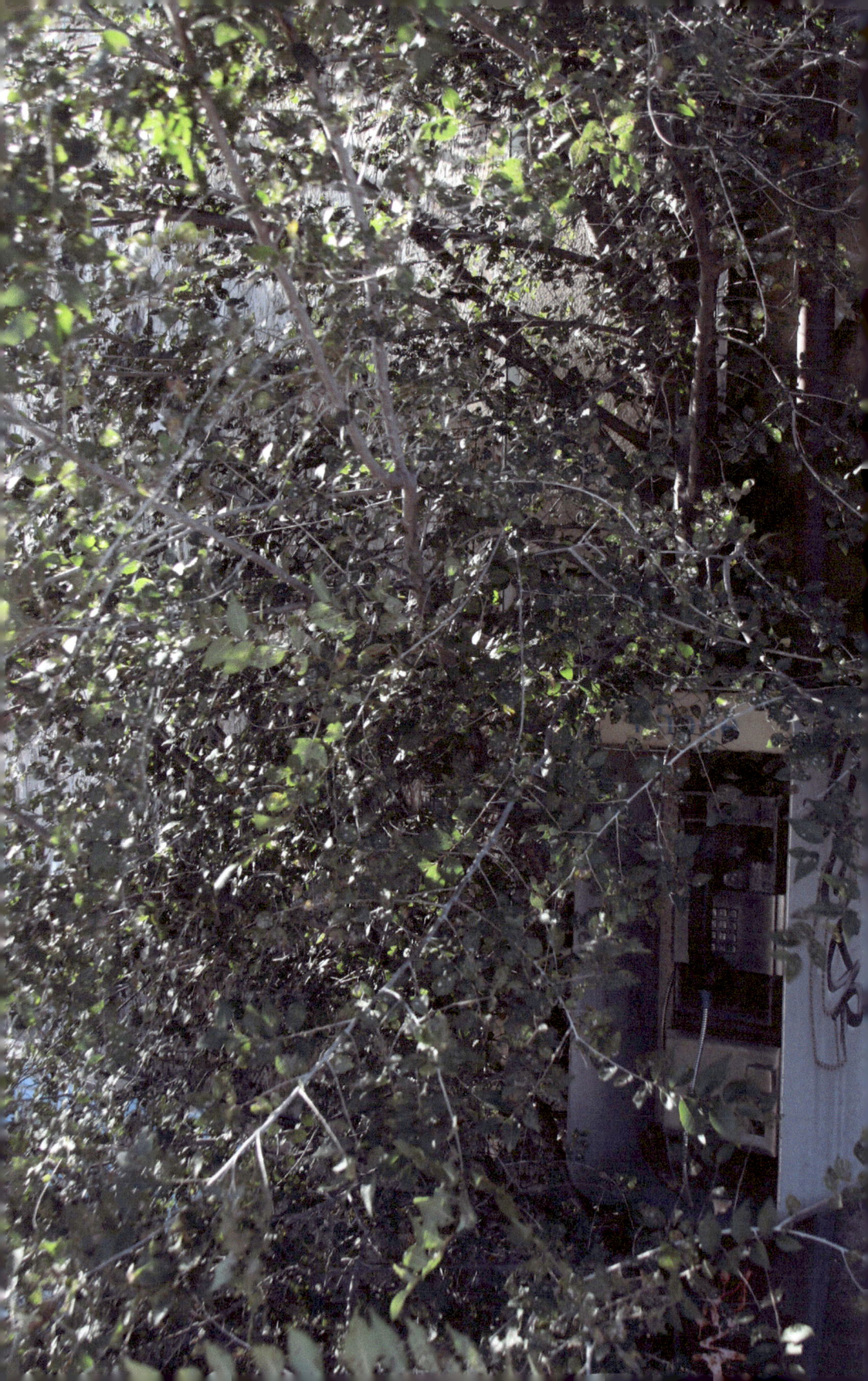

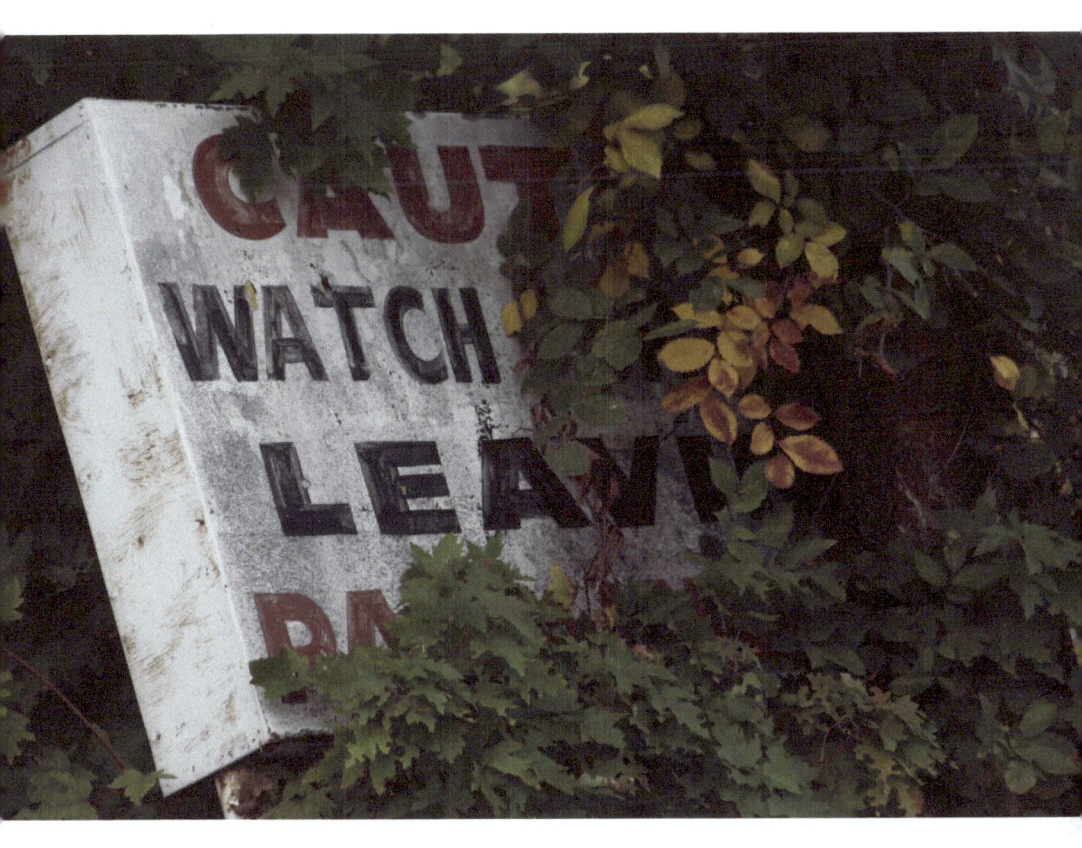

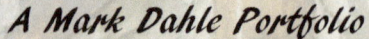

A Mark Dahle Portfolio

Amanda Gets A Pumpkin

(#1 in the series Amanda Wanted A Miracle)

This Mark Dahle Portfolio includes a colorful painting, twenty-four beautiful industrial photographs from Beijing, Shangahi and Xian, and a story about a girl who wanted a miracle.

"Oh dear," said her grandmother. "You didn't want a pumpkin? Perhaps we'll have to try again."

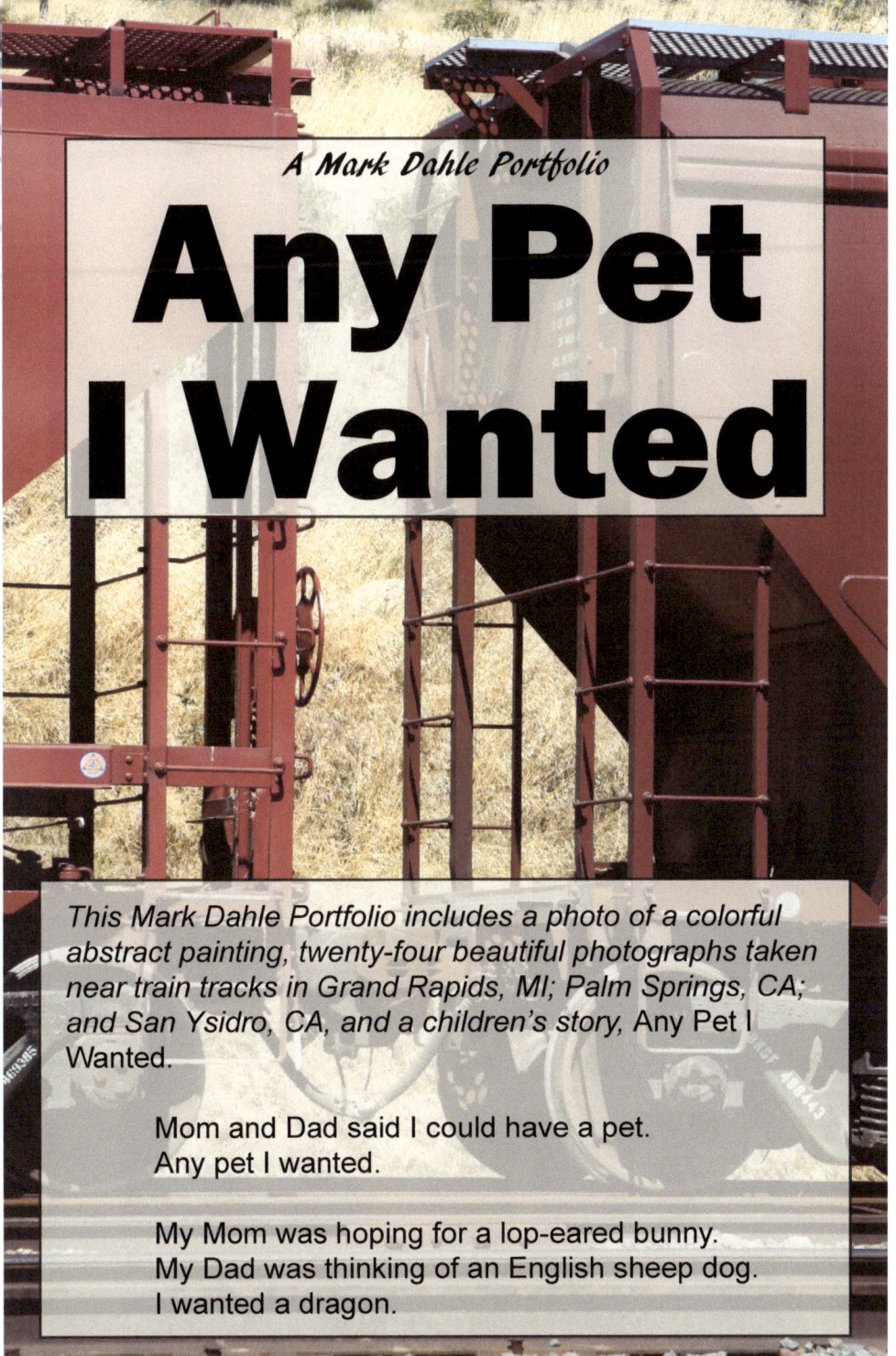

A Mark Dahle Portfolio

Any Pet I Wanted

This Mark Dahle Portfolio includes a photo of a colorful abstract painting, twenty-four beautiful photographs taken near train tracks in Grand Rapids, MI; Palm Springs, CA; and San Ysidro, CA, and a children's story, Any Pet I Wanted.

Mom and Dad said I could have a pet.
Any pet I wanted.

My Mom was hoping for a lop-eared bunny.
My Dad was thinking of an English sheep dog.
I wanted a dragon.

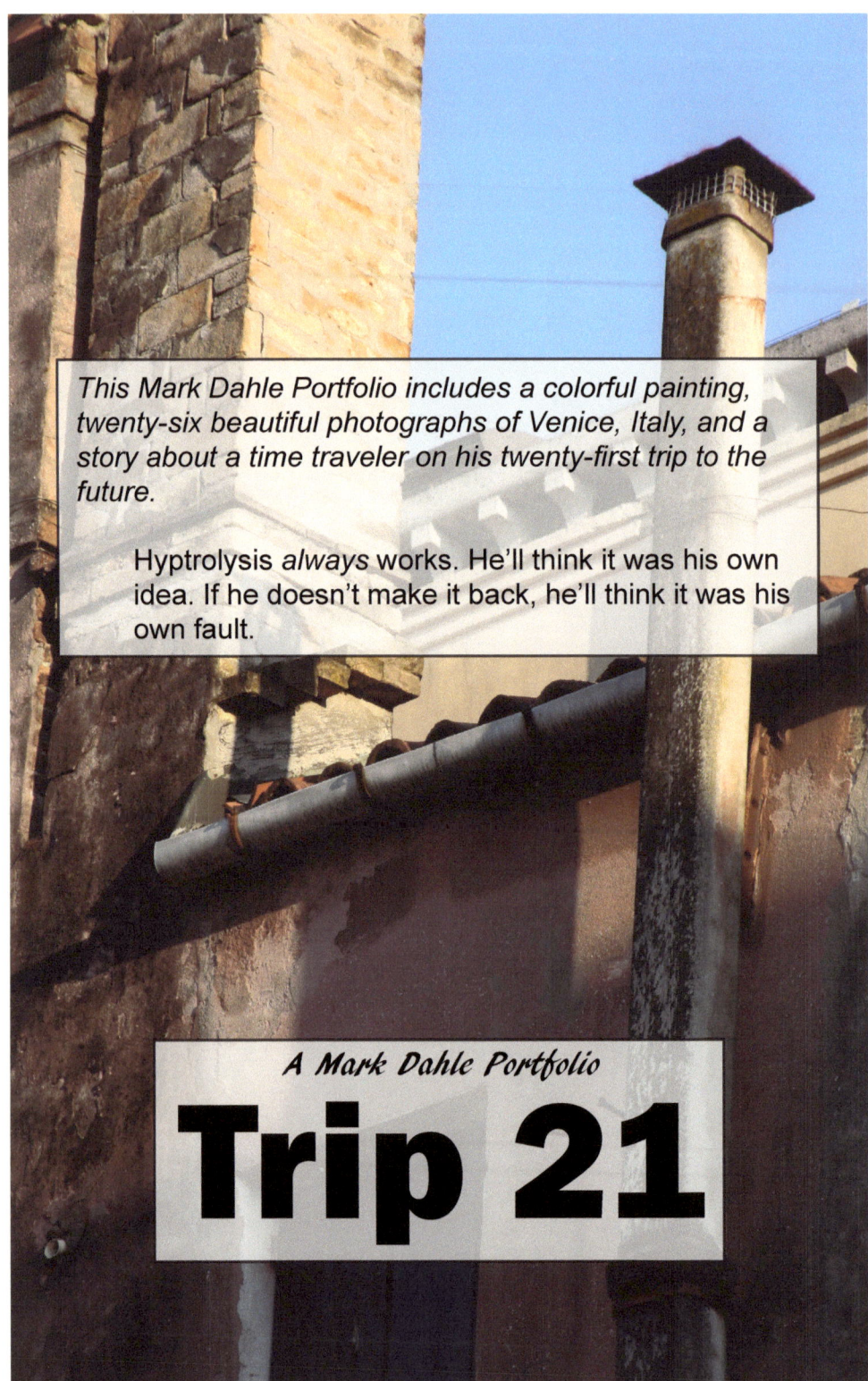

This Mark Dahle Portfolio includes a colorful painting, twenty-six beautiful photographs of Venice, Italy, and a story about a time traveler on his twenty-first trip to the future.

Hyptrolysis *always* works. He'll think it was his own idea. If he doesn't make it back, he'll think it was his own fault.

A Mark Dahle Portfolio

Trip 21

www.ingramcontent.com/pod-product-compliance
Lightning Source LLC
Chambersburg PA
CBHW040857180526
45159CB00001B/444